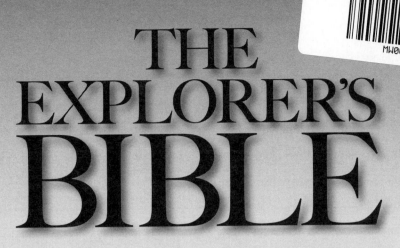

THE EXPLORER'S BIBLE

Volume 2: From Sinai to the Nation of Israel

Teacher's Lesson Plan Manual
By Lisa Bob Howard

24 Ready-to-Use Lesson Plans

Project Editor: Judy Dick
Design: Linda V. Curran
Copyright © 2011 Behrman House, Inc.
Springfield, New Jersey
ISBN: 978-0-87441-934-4 • Manufactured in the United States of America

Behrman House, Inc.
www.behrmanhouse.com

Contents

INTRODUCTION

The Explorer's Bible, Volume 2 invites students in grades 4 and 5 to continue their Bible study in a modern and accessible way. Each chapter leads students to explore the timeless traditions of the Bible text with a contemporary outlook and look to it for personal growth and values.

As Bible teachers, we join a long line of those who have ensured that our tradition is passed on from generation to generation. Through a rich and varied assortment of stories, discussions, and activities, *The Explorer's Bible 2* introduces students to a lifelong engagement with our most sacred text. Students are encouraged to learn from the great heroes of the Bible, as well as to learn from their mistakes. Above all, they are encouraged to make the lessons of the Bible a part of their own lives.

The eighteen chapters in *The Explorer's Bible, Volume 2* include biblical texts from the Book of Exodus through the Book of Ezra and Nehemiah. These chapters present the biblical accounts of the Israelites in the desert, establishing a kingdom in the Land of Israel, the exile to Babylonia, and the return to the Land of Israel. The **Table of Contents** (pages 4 -5) lists the title of each chapter and provides a visual clue for each one. You may wish to use it as an introduction with your students before reading each chapter or to review chapters the class has already studied.

Each chapter contains the following features:

- An **opening illustration** captures a key moment in the chapter.
- **Core text** presents translations and summaries of selected passages from the biblical text.
- **"Compass Notes"** in the margins expand on, explain, or pose questions based on the core text.

The Explorer's Bible, Volume 2 also contains recurring features that enrich the core text. These features, presented by cartoon "guides," are:

- **Midrash Maker** introduces students to classical midrashim from rabbinic and other sources and invites students to create their own midrashim.
- **Time Traveler** challenges students to imagine that they are present at the time of the story and to learn from biblical figures "firsthand."
- **Wisdom Weavers** summarizes and reinforces the main theme of the chapter. Following each Wisdom weaver is a visual activity that allows students to further explore the chapter's core concept.
- **Word Wizard** explores the meaning behind key Hebrew words and phrases.
- **The Tech Connection** provides suggestions for using the Internet to supplement the material covered in the lessons and for creating student work to be included in a class Web page or blog.

The **Timeline** (pages 157 – 159) provides students with a visual guide that places biblical events and personalities in a historical framework. Guide students to understand that there is much debate as to when various biblical events may have taken place.

STRUCTURE OF THIS LESSON PLAN MANUAL

This Lesson Plan Manual presents 24 ready-to-use lesson plans of approximately 45 – 60 minutes each for *The Explorer's Bible, Volume 2*. It includes suggestions for teaching the student text. In addition, ideas on how to incorporate technology are included in this introduction and in many of the lessons.

The chapters in the Lesson Plan Manual correspond to the chapters in the textbook and include one or two lesson plans. Each lesson plan includes the following elements:

- **Essential Question** An overarching question reflecting the main idea of the lesson.
- **Learning Objectives** Goals for students to achieve by the end of the chapter.
- **Getting Started** A set induction to get students thinking about the ideas they will learn in the lesson.
- **Exploring the Text** A step-by-step guide for presenting the lesson, including suggested activities and questions, as well as an approximate time frame for each section of the lesson.
- **Experiential Learning** Directions for an activity in which students learn through hands-on assignments.
- **Wrapping It Up** A short activity or discussion to review the main ideas of the lesson. Students reflect on the values learned in the lesson.

In addition to lesson plans, the Lesson Plan Manual provides suggestions for student assessment which can be found on page 32.

USING THIS LESSON PLAN MANUAL

At the start of the year, map out when you plan to teach each lesson. The 24 lessons in the manual have been designed so that you can teach an average of one lesson per week. Heighten student interest and engagement by scheduling additional time for incorporating technology into their Bible study.

Before you begin to teach a textbook chapter, read through the Lesson Plan Manual to familiarize yourself with the lesson plan. You may choose to use the lessons exactly as they are, or you may adapt the lessons to fit the needs of your students. If you adapt the lessons, it is important to frame your lesson around an essential question — either the one suggested for the lesson or another one that points to the main idea of the lesson.

The manual is easy to use with the student text. All references to readings, activities, and pictures are in bold, followed by the page number. For example, Lesson 1 recommends: Students read **Exodus 15:1–16:35** (page 11).

TEACHING STRATEGIES

Opening Rituals

1. Consider beginning each lesson with an opening ritual that signals to students that they are about to study an important text. A lovely and befitting ritual is to recite the blessing for engaging in learning Torah.

בָּרוּךְ אַתָּה יהוה אֱלֹהֵינוּ מֶלֶךְ הָעוֹלָם, אֲשֶׁר קִדְּשָׁנוּ בְּמִצְוֹתָיו וְצִוָּנוּ לַעֲסוֹק בְּדִבְרֵי תוֹרָה.

Praised are you, Adonai our God, Ruler of the world, who makes us holy with commandments and commands us to study words of Torah.

2. Conduct a brief review of the previous lesson. Students may play a simple review game, make a short presentation of the main ideas discussed, or share their answers to the previous lesson's Essential Question.

3. Post the Essential Question for the lesson to be studied on the board. Read the question aloud and discuss the meaning of the question, making sure students understand it.

Interpersonal and Intrapersonal Learners

Some students learn best through interacting with others (interpersonal); others learn best through working on their own (intrapersonal). With this in mind, the lessons offer activities for independent work, partner or group activities, and whole class projects. In general, if the manual does not specify that students are working individually, with partners or in a group, plan to have a class discussion.

Group Work

Group work can be a wonderful educational strategy. Many of the lessons include suggestions for group work. Whenever possible, plan ahead how you will form the groups. For some tasks, you will want students with a variety of talents and interests. For others, you may want to group together students with similar skills.

Group work is most successful when every member has a clear role. To make the group's task clear, prepare written instructions before class. In addition, you may want to create index cards that describe the jobs of group members. Jobs will vary depending on the type of group work.

Some possible jobs include the following:

- Recorder – records the group's suggestions or findings.
- Reporter – reports the group's work to the class.
- Reader – reads aloud the information to the group.
- Time Keeper – helps keep the group on task and keeps the group aware of how much time is left to complete the assignment.
- Illustrator – draws the group's ideas or completes visual tasks and presents them to class.

Reading the Text

The lesson plans vary the way the text is read so that students read on their own or aloud, with partners, or in groups. Most lessons include suggestions for more interactive techniques for reading the text aloud. This makes reading aloud more exciting for the students.

Student Journals

The lessons frequently include activities that require students to write responses to questions before they share answers with a partner, group, or the class. If possible, each student should have his or her own notebook that serves as a record of their answers and thoughts about the biblical stories and class discussions. Students can use this material to write blog entries before posting them on a class Web site.

Incorporating Maps

It will be helpful to have available a map of Israel and the Middle East from the biblical period. Identifying where events took place will enhance your students' understanding of biblical history as they study the Bible. If possible, also have available a modern map of Israel to use as a reference so that students can connect biblical events to modern-day Israel.

BEING INCLUSIVE

Like most classes, yours probably includes a diverse group of learners. Some students may require a variety of strategies or additional attention to be successful. The activities in this manual are intended for a wide spectrum of learners with a multitude of learning styles. By presenting material through a variety of modalities, you will have the greatest chance of reaching the most learners.

It is always helpful to find out from parents what accommodations, if any, their child's secular school makes. In addition, consider using one or several of the strategies below when you think they can address a particular learning need.

- Mask parts of the textbook so that only the activity being taught is visible. This can reduce distractions for some students and help them focus on the key lesson content.

- Highlight information in the text that students should pay close attention to.

- Help students share their learning in ways that are compatible with their learning styles. For example allow students to answer questions orally instead of writing their answers.

- Invite students to paraphrase or summarize what they have learned. This is helpful for all students.

- Allow some students extra time or reduce the number of items you expect them to complete.

- Repeat and define new words and concepts several times. Do not assume that students will recognize them when they see or hear them again later in the class session or in the next class.

- Create flashcards with key vocabulary words or concepts on one side and definitions on the other. Invite students to take them home to practice with a parent.

- Some activities will be especially engaging for students with special interests, such as art activities. Allow extra time for students to expand on these activities and encourage them to continue the project at home and post it on the class Web site or blog.

- Set up all students to succeed. When creating a group, make sure that all students can make contributions to the group. You may need to adapt the learning experience for some students with specific learning needs.

- Reach out to your director of education for support and guidance.

Most important, remember that the interpersonal relationships you build and the atmosphere of inclusiveness you create in your classroom are as important as the material you teach. At all times, try to model and encourage the qualities of patience and tolerance in all of your students. When we interact compassionately and justly with our students, we are bringing to life the teachings of the Bible.

EXPERIENTIAL LEARNING

Experiential learning processes engage the students in active, hands-on learning that deepens understanding and connection to the material. Experiential learning means learning by doing. For example, rather than reading about ways that Jewish children help others, students might volunteer at a shelter or run a winter coat drive.

The experiential education process generally includes three steps:

1. **Planning** This may include reading the Biblical text for necessary background information, having a class discussion about possible solutions, and creating individual or group plans to be carried out.
2. **Experiential Activity** Possible activities include field trips, putting on a play, learning a song, creating an art project, role playing, building, or planting.
3. **Review** After the students have completed their project, discuss the entire process. Encourage students to share their observations, insights and conclusions.

THE TECH CONNECTION

Your students are growing up in a world in which using technology is part of their daily lives at home and at school. There are infinite ways that you can take advantage of the internet and digital applications to deepen understandings, and to add creativity, interactivity, and excitement to your lessons.

Direct your students only to Web sites that you have previewed and approved. Some of the lessons call for students to run internet searches. This should only be done with teacher supervision to direct students to appropriate sites and images. When searches are suggested, search terms are included that have a high likelihood of returning appropriate sites and images. Adapt activities depending on the availability of computers in your classroom.

Consider creating a class Web site or blog with your students. If your congregation has a Web site, find out if your class can have space on it. Alternatively, there are instructions on the internet for creating your own Web site or blog. Students can update it weekly with new content, images, and their reactions to what they learned. Students might work on the Web site if they are early to school or have finished an assignment early. You might also designate class time for groups of students to work on the Web site.

The following suggestions will help you use a class Web site or blog to enhance student learning:

- Upload photographs or videos of students engaged in activities from the lessons in this manual.
- Post a survey question for parents based on a value in the chapter, then tally and share the results.
- Start a timeline using the one at the back of *The Explorer's Bible 2* as a guide. Update your class's timeline after you complete each chapter.
- Upload maps that show the changes in Israel's borders and the nations that ruled over the Land of Israel.
- Post students' responses to writing prompts in the lessons.
- Create fake social media pages for some of the characters in the Bible. Students might create a simulated Facebook profile for Samson or a Twitter feed for Jonah.
- Upload student artwork created in classroom activities from the lessons in this manual.

1 – The Great Miracle, Lesson 1

Essential Question: When should we make decisions based upon faith in God and ourselves?

Learning Objectives: Students will be able to:
- Describe the challenges the Israelites faced in the Sinai Desert and how they found the courage to move forward.
- Evaluate situations to determine whether we should take a leap of faith and act.
- Identify the biblical source for the Mi Chamocha prayer.

Getting Started: (5 minutes)

Students identify the miracle portrayed in the picture on pages 6-7. Explain that through this lesson, students will gain new understanding of a familiar story. Create a three-column **Know – Want to Know – Learned** chart on the board and have students brainstorm what they **Know** and **Want** to Know about the crossing of the Sea of Reeds.

Exploring the Text:
1. (15 minutes) Assign students to play the parts of the narrator, Pharaoh, Pharaoh's soldiers, God, the Israelites, and Moses for a dramatic reading of **Exodus 13:17–14:9** (page 7) and **Exodus 14:10–14:31** (pages 8-10). Place sheets of paper on the floor to represent the Sea of Reeds. Students act out the events in the front of the classroom with the narrator staying seated. Pharaoh and his soldiers should start in a far corner of the room. Ask: Why were the Israelites so afraid? Look at the picture on page 8. What might have given them the courage to keep moving forward? Do you think you would have had the courage to journey through the Sinai Desert?

2. (10 minutes) Divide students into groups of three. Each group selects a reader, writer, and a reporter. Groups read **The Long Way Home** (page 9). Students debate each suggestion and select one as their favorite. Reporters from each group share the group's choice and reasons with the class.

3. (10 minutes) Read aloud **The Faith of One** (page 12). Students complete the chart on page 13 individually. Read each item aloud and ask for students to raise their hands if they think it requires a leap of faith. Discuss their responses and more examples of situations they think require a leap of faith.

Experiential Learning: (10 minutes)

Students read **Exodus 15:1–16:35** (page 11) silently. Students locate Mi Chamocha in prayer books. Inform students that this is sung daily before the Amidah in the morning and evening prayer services. Sing it together as a class. Sing it again with students playing tambourines or other small instruments. Ask how the mood of the prayer changes when we add instruments.

The Tech Connection: (5 minutes)

Have several students use digital cameras to record videos of the students acting out the story. Post the videos on your class Web site or blog.

Wrapping It Up: (5 minutes)

Return to the **K – W – L** chart. Have each student add at least one thing they Learned. Students discuss how reading the texts and doing the activities added to their understanding of the story.

2 – God's Gift, Lesson 1
Essential Question: What does it mean to be holy?

Learning Objectives: Students will be able to:

- Retell the story of the giving of the commandments in their own words.
- Identify commandments that are rules between people and God and ones that are rules between people.
- Understand why holidays and ritual objects are called holy.

Getting Started: (5 minutes)

Show students a picture of a classroom, a sports stadium, and an orchestra hall. Ask: What are rules of behavior for each of these places? How do the rules differ for each place? Why does each place have special rules? What would happen if there were no rules? Explain that in this chapter, students will read about how the Israelites received God's laws at Mount Sinai. Ask students why the Israelites need rules at this point in their history.

Exploring the Text:

1. (15 minutes) Write the following three questions and instructions for reading on slips of paper:
   - Why were the Israelites brought to a mountain in the Sinai Desert? (Read **Exodus 19:1–6**, page 15)
   - Why did God give the people special instructions to get ready for getting the commandments? (Read **Exodus 19:10–14**, page 15)
   - What was the experience like for the people at Mount Sinai? (Read **Exodus 19:16–20:1**, page 16)

   Divide the class into groups of four. Each group receives a slip of paper and reads the relevant text. Students answer their question. Groups choose a representative from their group to present their reading and answer to the class.

2. (10 minutes) Read aloud the Ten Commandments listed in **Exodus 20:2–14** (page 16). Make two columns on the board. Ask: Which commandments are laws between God and people and which are laws between people and people? Write down their answers in the columns on the board. Ask: Which do you consider to be the most important commandment? Students suggest ideas for an eleventh commandment.

Experiential Learning: (15 minutes)

Read aloud **Holy, Holy, Holy** (page 20). Discuss how holiness is related to being set apart. Ask: What Jewish laws and customs require us to set things apart (*kashrut, Shabbat*)? Which of our customs makes us different from other nations (*hanging a mezuzah*)? How do these practices help us keep our Jewish identities strong? Ask students to identify objects that are holy and explain how they are set apart (*the Torah is kept in its own special place*).

The Tech Connection: (5 minutes)

Update the class Web site or blog with student ideas for an eleventh commandment. Invite parents to post comments with their ideas for an eleventh commandment.

Wrapping It Up: (10 minutes)

Ask: What does it means to be a "treasured people and a holy nation?" Working individually, students complete **A Picture of Holiness** (page 21) and integrate some of their answers into their scene.

2 – God's Gift, Lesson 2

Essential Question: How do people react to difficult situations and handle the consequences of their actions?

Learning Objectives: Students will be able to:

- Retell the story of the golden calf from the point of view of Moses, Aaron, and the Israelites.
- Compare and contrast the Israelites' mood and actions the first time Moses went up the mountain and returned with the second time he went up the mountain and returned.
- Provide explanations why Aaron made the golden calf.

Getting Started: (5 minutes)

Tell students that you will give them writing prompt. Upon hearing the prompt, they should write continuously for three minutes. Prompt: I am angry when… Explain that they will read about Moses, Aaron, and the Israelites coping with difficult emotions and how they handled these feelings.

Exploring the Text:

1. (15 minutes) Students should imagine that they are Israelites at Mount Sinai and keep a diary about the events that happened. They should write an entry in their journal at each prompt. Read aloud Exodus **24:12–18** (page 18). Prompt: Your leader has been gone for forty days — how do you feel? Continue reading **Exodus 32:1–6** (page 18). Prompt: Now you have an idol made of gold — how do you feel?

   Read **Exodus 32:15–20** (page 18). Prompt: You have seen your leader smash God's tablets. You have been punished. How do you feel? Read **Exodus 34:1–4, 28–32** (page 18). Prompt: Your leader has been gone another 40 days. Now he returns with a new set of tablets from God. How do you feel?

2. (15 minutes) Have students create "torn-paper midrash." Students divide a piece of colored construction paper in half and use torn pieces of colored paper to create an abstract picture on each half of the paper. The first half of the paper represents the events and mood the first time Moses went up the mountain and returned. The second half represents the events and mood the second time Moses went up the mountain and returned. Students show their work and discuss the differences between the two time periods.

3. (5 minutes) Partners read **The Righteous Women** (page 19) and answer the questions in the book.

Experiential Learning: (10 minutes)

Assign students to play the roles of Aaron and Moses. Students interview Aaron about his role in the story of the golden calf and Moses about his reactions to the golden calf.

Wrapping It Up: (5 minutes)

Students share examples of times they had to deal with difficult situations and their personal responses to them.

3 – The Courage of Two, Lesson 1

Essential Question: How do courage and optimism help us achieve our goals?

Learning Objectives: Students will be able to:

- Explain reasons why God had the Israelites wander in the desert for forty years.
- Compare and contrast the courage and optimism of Caleb and Joshua with the fear and negativity of the other scouts.
- Describe the events that prevented Moses from entering the land of Canaan.

Getting Started: (5 minutes)

Students consider how to choose a sleep-away camp for the summer. Ask: What would you want to know about the camp? What would make you decide on a specific camp? How would you get information about the camp? Students discuss how to evaluate what their friends say about the camps.

Exploring the Text:

1. (15 minutes) Students silently read **Numbers 13:1–20** (page 23). Students write down the information that Moses asked the scouts to find out about on their tour of the land of Canaan.

    Students continue to read **Numbers 13:25–33** (page 23) silently and add the scouts' answers to Moses' questions. Discuss the different answers and compare and contrast what Caleb and Joshua had to say with the statements of the other scouts.

    Ask for a show of hands to see who thinks the Israelites will believe the ten scouts and who thinks the Israelites will believe Caleb and Joshua.

2. (20 minutes) Divide students into four groups. Groups prepare dramatic presentations of one of the passages on pages 24 and 25 and perform them in front of the class. Ask: Why should the Israelites have faith in God? How many people who witnessed the plagues in Egypt will enter the land of Canaan? How might the people who left Egypt be different from their children who were born free?

Experiential Learning: (10 minutes)

Working individually, students read **A Chat with Moses** (page 26) and answer the questions as they think Moses might.

The Tech Connection: (10 minutes)

Teach students the Hebrew words for "a land flowing with milk and honey," *Eretz Zavat Halav U'devash*. Students search for photos of Israel on the internet to illustrate this biblical quote and create an on-line travel ad for biblical Israel.

> **Wrapping It Up:** (10 minutes)
> Read **Positive Power** (page 28) aloud. Discuss with students how seeing things in a positive light helps you achieve goals.

4 – Joshua Fights for Freedom, Lesson 1

Essential Question: What are the rewards and responsibilities that freedom brings?

Learning Objectives: Students will be able to:

- Identify the three sections of the Tanach.

- Dramatize the story of the battle of Jericho.

- Describe the blessings and responsibilities the Israelites received.

Getting Started: (10 minutes)

Make 3 columns on the board; Torah – Prophets – Writings. Explain to students that the Bible or Tanach is divided into three sections. Students suggest characters and events for each section. Add their suggestions to each column. Inform students that the Book of Joshua is the first book in Prophets. Ask: Why do you think Prophets starts with the Book of Joshua?

Exploring the Text:

1. (5 minutes) Read **Joshua 1:1–9** (page 31) aloud. Focus students' attention on God's directive that Joshua must follow the Teaching in order to prosper. Ask: What is the Teaching that Joshua must follow?

2. (20 minutes) Create the wall of the city of Jericho out of boxes or blocks on a desk at the front of the classroom. Leave an opening for the gate and assign one box to be Rahab's house. Select students to act out the following parts and give them puppets or dolls to represent the characters (except for God): God, Joshua, two spies, Rahab, and two soldiers. Read **Joshua 2:1** (page 31), **Joshua 2:2–7** (page 32), and **Joshua 2:8–15** (page 32) aloud. Have the selected students read their parts and dramatize the actions of their characters as you read.

   Cover the opening in the city's wall. Choose two students to act as the troops walking around the city and one to act for the priests. Tell the class they should respond as the Israelites. Read **Joshua 6:1–5** (page 32) and **Joshua 6:8–24** (page 35). Students act out the story. Carefully bring down the walls of the city.

   Ask: Why do you think God tells Joshua to have the troops march around Jericho for seven days? Why would God command Joshua to have the priests circle the city on the seventh day blowing horns? Why include the Ark of the Covenant (which contained the tablets) with them? How is the conquering of Jericho a joint effort between God and the Israelites?

Experiential Learning: (10 minutes)

Students read **God's Reminder** (page 36) silently. Students write down what freedom means for them personally. Discuss their definitions and identify rewards and responsibilities that would be the result of having that freedom.

The Tech Connection: (5 minutes) Students find the Jewish Museum's website at http://www.thejewishmuseum.org/onlinecollection/browse.php. Students search in the museum's on-line collections for the painting "The Taking of Jericho." Students give descriptive words for the mood of the painting. Discuss how the artist chose to depict this event.

Wrapping It Up: (5 minutes)

Explain that once the Israelites enter Canaan, they had more freedom as well as the blessings and responsibilities that come with that freedom. Ask: What are the blessings that the Israelites have received? What are the responsibilities?

5 – Deborah's Help, Lesson 1
Essential Question: Why is it important to have good leaders?

Learning Objectives: Students will be able to:

- Identify qualities of a good leader.

- Explain the role of a biblical judge.

- Learn what goes into making good decisions.

Getting Started: (10 minutes)
As a class, students write a "Help Wanted" ad for the next leader after Joshua. Ad should include a job description, required qualifications, and any other relevant details. Use the ad to discuss the kind of leader needed for the Israelites after Joshua.

Exploring the Text:

1. (10 minutes) Students read silently **Joshua 23:1–24:29** (page 39) and write questions for Joshua that they think the Israelites should have asked. Students should consider what information would be helpful to the Israelites when Joshua would no longer be there to lead them. Students share their questions with the class. Ask: Why does Joshua tell the Israelites the history of their ancestors?

2. (10 minutes) Students read **Judges 2:10–3:31** (page 40) and the corresponding compass note on page 40 silently. Ask: Why do you think the Israelites were able to defeat their enemies and have periods of peace when they had a judge? Students compare and contrast the leadership qualities of biblical judges to the "Help Wanted" ad that was created by the class.

Experiential Learning: (15 minutes)
Read **Judges 4:1–5** (page 40) aloud. Assign a student to role-play Deborah. Give "Deborah" a special place to sit. Ask the other students to think of decisions for which an Israelite may have sought the help of a judge. Invite students to come up one at a time to ask for help with their decisions. Ask: How did it feel to have someone else make a decision? How did it feel to be the one responsible for guiding other's choices? Have different students take on the role of Deborah.

The Tech Connection: (10 minutes)
Partners work together to create a Facebook-like profile for Deborah. Students should include job, religious views, and activities and interests in the profile. They should also draw a picture of what they think Deborah looked like for the profile. Post on your class Web site or blog.

> **Wrapping It Up:** (5 minutes)
> Read aloud the first comment on page 41 and accompanying question. Students discuss their thoughts about how Deborah's decisions may have been influenced by the Torah.

5 – Deborah's Help, Lesson 2

Essential Question: In what way does working with others help us achieve our goals?

Learning Objectives: Students will be able to:

- Identify examples from the text of people working together.

- Describe female role models in the Bible.

- Demonstrate how words and phrases are repeated in biblical poetry.

Getting Started: (5 minutes)

Students write about a time they asked another person for help or a time when asking someone for help would have made a task easier. Tell students that in this lesson, they will read about how a battle was won by people working together.

Exploring the Text:

1. (5 minutes) Choose two students to read the lines of Deborah and Barak. Read aloud **Judges 4:6–9** (page 40) Ask: Why do you think Barak would not go without Deborah? How do you think Barak felt when he heard Deborah's response?

    Experiential Learning: (10 minutes) Have several volunteers stand on one side of the classroom. Instruct them to close their eyes and walk to the other side of the room. Ask: How hard or easy was it to do this activity? Assign each of the volunteers a partner from the rest of the class and instruct them to walk across the room again in pairs, with one partner's eyes shut and the other partner's eyes open. Discuss which round was easier and why.

2. Ask a student to read **Help!** (page 44). Ask: How did this activity illustrate the ideas on this page and how does it relate to the story of Deborah?

3. (15 minutes) Read **Judges 4:14–21** (page 41) aloud. Ask: Why do you think Yael killed Sisera? Partners write down descriptive words for the qualities of Deborah and Yael and share their answers with the class. Ask: How can Deborah and Yael serve as role models? Have students create a "Bible Hero Card" in the model of a baseball card for either Deborah or Yael. Display the cards in the classroom.

4. (10 minutes) Read **Judges 5:1–31** (page 42) aloud. Ask: What makes this piece of writing a poem? Tell students that poetry often uses words and phrases that sound similar to each other. Ask: Which words or phrases sound similar to "God of Israel"? What words are repeated? Why do you think these words are repeated?

The Tech Connection: (10 minutes)

Partners work together to add to the Facebook-like profile they created for Deborah. Students should include job and activity updates to the profile. Post on your class Web site or blog.

> **Wrapping It Up:** (5 minutes)
> Read **A Clean Start** (page 42). Ask: What kind of leader would you choose to lead the people in Israel after Deborah?

6 – Samson's Purpose, Lesson 1
Essential Question: How can we each make contributions to the world?

Learning Objectives: Students will be able to:

- Explain the source of Samson's strength.
- Creatively retell the story of Samson.
- Generate ideas for how we can each make a contribution to the world.

Getting Started: (5 minutes)

Give each student a piece of colored paper and instruct them to draw an outline of a human figure on it. Students write suggestions on their picture to show how different parts of the body can be used to help the world. On the hands, they write how they can use their hands to improve the world. On the eyes, students write how they can use their eyes to improve the world, and so on. Explain that in this lesson, they will learn about the hero Samson who had a special purpose in the world.

Exploring the Text:

1. (30 minutes) Divide students into groups of four students each. Assign each group passages from pages 47- 50. Instruct the groups to read their passages together and prepare a segment for the news that retells their part of the story. They should imagine that they are living at the time of the events in their passages. They can include interviews, live action "footage," and on-site reporting. Each segment should take several minutes. Have groups perform their news pieces in the correct order for the rest of the class.

   Hold a class discussion about the story of Samson. Ask: What do you think it means to have the spirit of God? Does Samson behave as you would expect a person who has the spirit of God in him to behave? Why do you think Samson lies to Delilah? What is the source of Samson's strength? What do we learn about Samson's dedication to God and the Israelites?

Experiential Learning: (10 minutes)

Students read **Purpose Puzzle** (page 52) silently. As a class, develop a plan for a class project that would help make the world more peaceful using the individual strengths and interests of the students. Students may draw upon the ideas they generated during the **Getting Started** part of the lesson.

The Tech Connection: (10 minutes)

Students imagine that Samson's story takes place in modern times and write a Twitter feed for him at different points in the story. Students post their tweets on the class Web site or blog.

> **Wrapping It Up:** (5 minutes)
> Students read **A Peace of the Puzzle** (page 53) silently and complete the activity. Students add details to the section about themselves about how they can make a contribution to the world.

7 – Ruth's Choice, Lesson 1
Essential Question: How are all kinds of Jews part of the Jewish community?

Learning Objectives: Students will be able to:

- Do a close reading of the story of Ruth choosing to stay with Naomi.

- Interpret Ruth's statement, "Your people will be my people, and your God my God."

- Describe at least three ways in which all Jews share in the Covenant and traditions of our people.

Getting Started: (5 minutes)
Look at the picture of the different *mezuzot* on page 60. Read the caption aloud. Ask: In what ways can Jews be different from each other?

Exploring the Text:

1. (10 minutes) Partners do a close reading of **Ruth 1:1–5** and **Ruth 1:6–19** (page 55). Direct the pairs to make a list of questions about the story told in the text. Partners choose one of their questions to share with the class. Volunteers offer answers to the questions.

2. (5 minutes) Remind students that Abraham, like Ruth, left his home to go to the land of Israel (then Canaan). Have students compare and contrast Abraham's move with Ruth's move. Discuss the difference between being told by God to move (Abraham) and making your own decision to go (Ruth).

3. (5 minutes) Direct students' attention to the phrase, "Your people will be my people, and your God my God." Ask: What do you think this statement means? Why did Ruth make this pledge? Read **Your People Will Be My People** (page 56) aloud.

4. (10 minutes) Inform students that tradition teaches us we are forbidden to remind a convert of his or her former status. Like Ruth, once a person converts to Judaism, he or she is just as Jewish as anyone born a Jew. Have students work individually to complete **We've All Got A Share** (page 61).

Experiential Learning: (5 minutes)
Have students locate the thirteenth blessing *Al hatzadikim* in the traditional weekday Amidah. Read this blessing aloud in English. Ask students to name the groups of people for whom we are asking God to be merciful. Based on this prayer, what is the Jewish attitude towards converts?

The Tech Connection: (10 minutes)
Students write a journal entry about their own family's Jewish history and customs and post entries on the class Web site or blog.

> **Wrapping It Up:** (5 minutes)
> Remind students that at the beginning of the lesson, we talked about ways in which Jews are different. Ask: What do Jews of all kinds have in common with each other?

7 – **Ruth's Choice**, Lesson 2
Essential Question: How can we help people in need?

Learning Objectives: Students will be able to:

- Map out the story of Ruth and Boaz.

- Suggest ways that we can help others in need.

- Describe ways in which Ruth can serve as a role model for us.

Getting Started: (5 minutes)

Students look at the photo on page 57 while one person reads **Ruth 1:22–2:3** (page 56) and the photo caption aloud. Tell students about the laws regarding leaving grain for the poor (Leviticus 19:22). Ask: How can those of us who do not live on a farm help the poor today?

Exploring the Text:

1. (10 minutes) One student reads aloud the first two sentences of **Ruth 2:5–12** (page 56). Students write their own predictions for how Boaz will treat Ruth. Share predictions. Have the student finish reading the paragraph and compare students' predictions to what happened. Ask: What impresses Boaz about Ruth? Assign another student to read **Ruth 2:18–20** and **Ruth 3:1–7** (page 57). Students write individual predictions for how Boaz will respond when he sees Ruth. Share predictions.

2. (10 minutes) Partners create story maps on blank construction paper to keep track of the characters and events in this chapter. Instruct students to record characters, important events, and outcomes.

3. (10 minutes) Partners read **Ruth 3:8–13** and Ruth **4:1–11** (page 58) together and add to their story map. Read **Ruth 4:13–17** (page 58) aloud. Why is this genealogy information included? What was the final outcome of Ruth's good deeds?

Experiential Learning: (15 minutes)

Students create their own tzedakah boxes to take home. Provide students with small cardboard boxes, metal cans, or glass jars to decorate. Students cut and paste images from magazines to create decoupage illustrations on their containers that reflect their own ideas about tzedakah.

The Tech Connection: (5 minutes)

Divide students into small groups. Groups create a PowerPoint slide that summarizes the story of Ruth and Boaz using graphics and bullet points. Print the slides and compile them into a book. Discuss how the groups represented the story.

Wrapping It Up: (5 minutes)

In an earlier lesson about Samson, students developed a plan that would make the world a better place. Ask: Have you taken any steps towards making your plan a reality? How can you improve your efforts? What lessons can you learn from Ruth?

---

8 – Samuel and the King, Lesson 1

Essential Question: When should we follow the crowd and when should we find our own way?

Learning Objectives: Students will be able to:

- Recount the story of Samuel's birth and Saul's rise to power.

- Present arguments for and against the Israelites having a king.

- List criteria that help us decide if we should follow the crowd or determine our own path.

Getting Started: (5 minutes) Students brainstorm words that describe a king. Write all ideas on the board. Students consider the list and identify words that contradict each other. Ask: What do you think should be the role of a king? Return to the list and evaluate whether the descriptive words reflect how they think a king acts.

Exploring the Text:

1. (20 minutes) Divide students into groups of three or four. Students decide who will be the recorder, reporter, and reader. Explain to students that they will be creating an argument for whether the Israelites should have a king or not. Assign half the groups to be in favor of a king and half to be against having a king.

2. Students read **1 Samuel 1:1–28**, **1 Samuel 2:1–10**, **1 Samuel 3:1–20**, **1 Samuel 8:4-9**, and **1 Samuel 8:10–22; 9:15–16** (pages 63 and 64) in their groups. The pro-king groups create posters listing arguments in favor of the Israelites having a king, while the con groups create posters listing arguments against Israel having a king. Groups presents their posters and students vote on whether the Israelites should have a king or not.

3. (10 minutes) Assign students to read the roles of Saul, the servant, Samuel, and the people. Read aloud **1 Samuel 9:1–10**, **1 Samuel 9:19–10:1** (page 65), and **1 Samuel 10:17–24** (page 67). Working individually, students complete **Super Saul** (page 66).

4. (5 minutes) Students take turns reading aloud the passages **1 Samuel 13:1–9 and 1 Samuel 13:10–14; 15:10–11** (page 67). Remind them that in the beginning of a blessing, we refer to God as *Melech ha'olam* which means "Ruler of the Universe." Ask: How does this information inform the arguments in favor of and against the Israelites having a king?

Experiential Learning: (10 minutes) Students read **Follow the Crowd?** (page 68) silently. Students consider the following scenarios and decide whether they would follow the crowd or create their own path.

- Friends are going to an R-rated movie.

- Friends are playing sports with a group of children who have special needs.

- Friends are stealing art supplies from school.

- Friends are volunteering to help clean up the school on a Sunday.

- Friends are making fun of a student for wearing an out-of-style shirt.

  Discuss their answers.

The Tech Connection: (10 minutes) Partners create a PowerPoint presentation that teaches others how to know when to follow a crowd or make independent decisions.

Wrapping It Up: (5 minutes)
Complete **Join or Walk** Away (page 69) individually. Share ideas as a class.

---

9 – David's Friends and Foes, Lesson 1

Essential Question: How are the rewards of friendship uniquely precious?

Learning Objectives: Students will be able to:

- Explain how David came to be king of Israel.

- Describe David's relationship with Saul and Saul's children, Jonathan and Michal.

- Artistically portray the character of David.

Getting Started: (5 minutes)

On a piece of paper, students rank the following items (with the most important first): Immediate Family, Group of Friends, Personal Goals, Best Friend, Hobbies, Distant Relatives. Ask: Was this easy or difficult? What did you rank first? What did you rank last? Where does your best friend fall in your list? Explain that in this chapter, students will learn of the famous friendship between Jonathan, Saul's son, and David.

Exploring the Text:

1. (5 minutes) Read **1 Samuel 17:1–7** (page 71) aloud. Ask: How is Goliath described? Why is he described in such detail?

2. (10 minutes) Assign students to act out the roles of Narrator, Goliath, Saul, and David in front of the class. Read **1 Samuel 17:8–32, 1 Samuel 16:21–23; 17:33–37, 1 Samuel 17:40–48** (page 72) and **1 Samuel 17:49–18:2** (page 74). Students act out the story as it is read.

3. (5 minutes) Students read 1 Samuel 18:5-7, **1 Samuel 18:8–9**, and **1 Samuel 18:1–3, 20–29** (page 75) silently. Ask: Was Saul justified in being suspicious of David?

4. (10 minutes) Partners read **1 Samuel 19:9–20, 1 Samuel 20:28–35, 1 Samuel 20: 41–42**, and **1 Samuel 21:1–2 Samuel 5:5** (page 76). Students discuss how they would describe the friendship between Jonathan and David. Partners read **Friends Forever** (page 78).

Experiential Learning: (15 minutes)

Like many other biblical stories, this story has inspired a great deal of art. Using what they have learned about David, students work individually to create their own portrait of David. Provide students with a variety of materials such as fabric, buttons, colored paper, oil pastels, and markers.

The Tech Connection: (5 minutes)

Students search for the "Rothschild Miscellany" in Google Images. Students locate the image of King David and describe how David is shown in the painting. Point out that King David was a musician and poet and wrote much of the Book of Psalms. This picture is included in a unique Book of Psalms and contains the first word of the book.

> **Wrapping It Up:** (5 minutes)
> Go around the room and ask each student to give a reason why he or she thinks David was chosen to be the king of Israel.

10 – David Stands Guilty, Lesson 1
Essential Question: Why is it necessary to accept responsibility for one's actions?

Learning Objectives: Students will be able to:
- Creatively retell the story of King David and Batsheba.
- Evaluate King David's actions in this Biblical story.
- Discuss how the events in this chapter show the need to accept responsibility for our actions.

Getting Started: (5 minutes)

Give students the following scenario: During a test, George copies the work of the student sitting next to him. The next day, the teacher asks to see both students. Ask students to predict: What might happen if George admits his wrongdoing? If he lies to the teacher and gets caught?

Exploring the Text:

1. (5 minutes) Ask a volunteer to read **2 Samuel 6:1–17** (page 81). Show them Jerusalem on a map of Israel in King David's times and the photo of Jerusalem on pages 82-83. Read the caption and ask students to suggest reasons why conquering Jerusalem and bringing the Ark of the Covenant there was a brilliant military move. Students should take into account its location (*on the border of Judah and Northern Israel*), physical characteristics (*on a mountain*), and place amongst the Israelite tribes (*Jerusalem was not part of any tribe's land*).

2. (5 minutes) Students read **2 Samuel 7:4–29** (page 81) silently and underline in the text the promises God made to David.

3. (15 minutes) Read **2 Samuel 11:1–5** (page 82) aloud. Ask: What should David do now? What are the consequences of his actions?

   Read **2 Samuel 11:6–11** (page 83) aloud. Ask: What should David do now? What are the consequences of each action he might take? What do you think of Uriah? What do you think of David?

   Read **2 Samuel 11:14–27** (page 84) aloud. Ask: What do you think about what David did? Who is responsible for Uriah's death? Why was God angry?

   Read **2 Samuel 12:1–4** (page 84) aloud. Students interpret the parable by identifying who the rich man, the poor man, and the lamb represent. Ask: What is the message for King David?

Experiential Learning: (20 minutes)

Working individually, students create their own four-frame comic strip that retells the story up until this point. Partners read **2 Samuel 12:5–10** (page 85) and page 86. Ask: What can we learn from Nathan's words: "God will show you forgiveness because you accept responsibility for having done wrong?" Partners read **Who, Me?** (page 88). Students complete their comic strips by adding a fifth frame that concludes the story.

The Tech Connection: (10 minutes)

Students conduct a search for "City of David" in Google Images to find photos and maps of the area of Jerusalem that dates to King David's time. Direct students' attention to the historical importance of Jerusalem as the capital of ancient Israel.

Wrapping It Up: (5 minutes)
Ask: Are you surprised that the Bible includes this story? What other biblical figures made mistakes? How does it help us to read about the mistakes of others?

11 – **Solomon Chooses Wisdom**, Lesson 1
Essential Question: Why is it important to value wisdom?

Learning Objectives: Students will be able to:

- Describe the difference between wisdom, knowledge, and understanding.
- Classify choices as wise or unwise.
- List at least three places where "wisdom" is mentioned in the Tanach.

Getting Started: (5 minutes)

Write "Happy is the one who has found wisdom" (Proverbs 3:13) on the board. Students write a few sentences to explain what the proverb means. Discuss their ideas with the class. Ask: What is the difference between wisdom and knowledge? Do you know anyone who you consider wise?

Exploring the Text:

1. (5 minutes) Partners read **1 Kings 2:1–12** (page 91). Ask: What are some differences between how David became king and how Solomon became king?

2. (5 minutes) Students brainstorm a list of Biblical accounts in which God communicates through dreams. Read **1 Kings 3:5–15** (page 91) aloud. Explain that dreams in the Bible are related to prophecy and are considered a way to find out God's will. Ask: What do we learn about Solomon from his request?

3. (15 minutes) Read **1 Kings 3:16–22** (page 92) aloud. In groups of three or four, students develop solutions to the case before King Solomon and share their ideas with the class. The class votes for the best one. Read **1 Kings 3:24–28** (page 92) aloud. Ask: How does Solomon's solution show his wisdom? Read **1 Kings 5:9–14** (page 92) aloud. Ask: What is the difference between wisdom and understanding?

The Tech Connection: (10 minutes)

Students use an on-line Tanach (such as on Chabad.org; click on "library," then "classic texts," and then "The Complete Tanach") to search for the word "wisdom" in the Tanach. Students choose one of the many results from Proverbs and make a flyer with their quote to share with the class. Ask: Why do you think the word "wisdom" appears so many times in the Tanach?

Experiential Learning: (10 minutes)

Students complete **Wisdom's Way** (page 97) and then create their own maze using other wise and unwise choices. Students exchange mazes with each other. On the board make a list of wise and unwise choices that students included in their mazes. Discuss what constitutes a wise choice.

> **Wrapping It Up:** (5 minutes)
> Students write journal entries describing why wisdom is important and how they might make more wise choices in the future.

11 – Solomon Chooses Wisdom, Lesson 2

Essential Question: How can we make mitzvot (commandments) more special by using beautiful items?

Learning Objectives: Students will be able to:

- Evaluate Solomon's actions regarding the building of the Temple.
- Retell the midrash of the two brothers and the location of Solomon's Temple.
- Explain the concept of *hidur mitzvah*.

Getting Started: (5 minutes)
Show students photos of Torah Arks from different synagogues. Ask: Why do we keep the Torah in a special place? Would it matter if we kept it in a plain cardboard box?

Exploring the Text:

1. (10 minutes) Assign a student to read the first two sentences of **1 Kings 5:16–6:38** (page 93) and to then call on another student to continue reading. Finish reading the page in this way. Ask: What is a treaty? What do we learn about Solomon from the account of the treaty? Why does Solomon choose to build the Temple with gold and fine woods? Read **1 Kings 8:1–66** (page 95) aloud.

2. (5 minutes) Explain to the class that in Judaism there is a concept called *hidur mitzvah* in which a mitzvah (commandment) is made more special by using beautiful objects to fulfill it. Look at the picture on page 95 for an example. Ask: How does this object make Shabbat more special? Ask students to think of more examples.

Experiential Learning: (20 minutes)
Divide the class into groups of three or four. Give each group a paper bag of items that they must use in a play about the story of the two brothers. Students read **Holy Ground** (page 94) in their groups and create and perform their play for the class.

Point out to students that the name Solomon (Hebrew: Shlomo) is built on the root word shaleim which means "complete." It is the same root of the word shalom which means "peace," "hello," and "goodbye." Ask: What are the connections between the words shaleim, shalom, and Solomon?

The Tech Connection: (5 minutes)
Do a Google Image search for "Solomon's Temple model." Students write a journal entry describing what it might have been like to visit the Temple.

Wrapping It Up: (5 minutes)
Ask: How did Solomon make sure that the Temple was a uniquely special place to worship God?

12 – Elijah's Challenge, Lesson 1

Essential Question: How can we resist the temptation to put our faith in things we can see and touch?

Learning Objectives: Students will be able to:

- Describe the role of a prophet.
- Distinguish between the kingdom of Israel and the kingdom of Judah.
- Explain how to recognize and avoid our modern versions of "false idols."

Getting Started: (5 minutes)
Create a K-W-L chart on the board. Students create the same chart on a piece of paper. Students brainstorm everything they **K**now about the Prophet Elijah. Students list everything they **W**ant to know about Elijah.

Exploring the Text:

1. (10 minutes) A volunteer reads **1 Kings 12:1–20** (page 99). Show students a map of ancient Israel with the division between Judah and Israel. Have them find Jerusalem and the location of the Temple. Ask: How might this split into two kingdoms affect the worship of God among Israelites in the North?

   A volunteer reads **1 Kings 15:1–16:34** (page 99). Students look at the picture of the statue of Baal on page 100 and read the caption. Ask: Why do you think King Ahab worshipped Baal? Why do you think he was a terrible king?

2. (20 minutes) Divide students into groups and ask them to choose a recorder, reporter, illustrator, and reader. Students read **1 Kings 18:16–20** (page 99), **1 Kings 18:22–24** (page 101), and **1 Kings 18:26–29** (page 101) in their groups. Each group creates two newspaper ads encouraging people to come to the meeting of the prophets of Baal and the Prophet Elijah on Mount Carmel. One ad would run the day after Elijah issued the challenge to the prophets of Baal and the other would run several days later after the prophets had failed to start their fire. Share the ads with the class. Ask students to predict how the story will conclude. A volunteer reads **1 Kings 18:36–40** (page 101) aloud.

Experiential Learning: (15 minutes)
Students read **1 Kings 19:16–21** (page 101), **2 Kings 2:1–8** (page 102). **2 Kings 2:9–11** (page 102), and **2 Kings 2:13–15** (page 103) silently. Students each create a newspaper article that teaches about the role of a prophet and is based on any of the events in this chapter. The articles may include interviews, opinion pieces, and illustrations. Create a class newspaper that includes all the articles. Make copies for each student.

> **Wrapping It Up:** (5 minutes)
> A volunteer reads **Idol Chatter** (page 104). As a class, create a list of modern "false gods." Discuss how, like the Israelites, we can easily be influenced by those living around us. Students tell how we can avoid putting our faith in material things. Students finish their **K-W-L** charts, adding what they **L**earned.

13 – Jonah's Message, Lesson 1

Essential Question: Why are repentance and forgiveness important values?

Learning Objectives: Students will be able to:

- Describe some of the responsibilities of a prophet.

- Evaluate the choices available to Jonah, God, and the sailors throughout the story.

- Explain how the account of Jonah illustrates the Jewish values of repentance and forgiveness.

Getting Started: (5 minutes)

Students tell what they know of the story of Jonah. Explain that in this chapter they will be exploring the biblical account further by creating a simulation of the story.

Exploring the Text:

1. (10 minutes) Rearrange the classroom to simulate the ship. Assign students to be God, Jonah, and the captain. The rest of the class will be sailors. Read aloud the text as students act out the story. Read **Jonah 1:1–3, 1:4-6,** and **Jonah 1:7–11** (page 107). Freeze the scene.

2. (5 minutes) Students discuss what should be done to appease God. Debate the merits of throwing Jonah overboard, offering a community prayer, and other ideas. Students should try to reach an agreement.

3. (10 minutes) Students continue to simulate the story. Read **Jonah 1:11–16** (page 108). Designate an area of the classroom to represent the belly of the fish. Read **Jonah:1–11** (page 108). Ask: What did you like about the character you played? What did you dislike? Was it easy or difficult to come to an agreement for what to do with Jonah?

4. (10 minutes) Partners read **Jonah 3:1–10** (page 109). Students compare Jonah's response in Chapter 3 to his response in Chapter 1. Ask: How do Jonah and the Ninevites repent? Partners read **Jonah 4:1–4** (page 109). Ask: Why do you think Jonah is so upset? Are you surprised by his reaction?

Experiential Learning: (10 minutes)

Read **Jonah 4:5–9** (page 111) and the first compass note aloud. Students draw a picture of a *kikayon* plant using their imaginations. Ask students to crumple up their illustrations. Ask: What does it feel like when you destroy something that you created? Read **Jonah 4:10–11** (page 111) aloud. Ask: How does this activity help you understand God's explanation to Jonah for destroying the plant?

The Tech Connection: (5 minutes)

Students write a journal entry from the point of view of their character from the simulation and post it on the class Web site or blog.

> **Wrapping It Up:** (5 minutes)
> Read **A Stormy Story** (page 112) aloud. Brainstorm reasons to be forgiving. Ask: What do you think Jonah would say on the topic of forgiveness?

14 – Isaiah's World of Peace, Lesson 1
Essential Question: What can we do to create a better world?

Learning Objectives: Students will be able to:

- Visualize Isaiah's visions for a better world.

- Interpret poetic verses.

- Explain how the teachings of Isaiah are relevant today.

Getting Started: (5 minutes)

Draw a globe on the board. Ask a volunteer to draw and write students' ideas for what would be in their ideal world. Discuss what each student added to the vision. Explain that in this lesson, students will learn about the prophet Isaiah's perfect world.

Exploring the Text:

1. (5 minutes) Call on students to read the words of the two professors on page 115. Students look at the picture on page 114 and describe the image. Ask: What is unusual about the picture? Why is it an ideal image?

2. (10 minutes) Working individually, students draw a globe on a piece of colored paper and complete a picture of Isaiah's perfect world based on the poetic verses included in this chapter. They should include something from each quotation.

3. (10 minutes) Read **Isaiah 2:4** (page 116). Ask: Why would Isaiah want God to serve as a Judge? What would the world be like if people could "beat their swords into plowshares and their spears into pruning hooks?" Do we need to study about war today? Why?

   Read **Isaiah 11:1–6** (page 117) and the compass note aloud. Ask: What qualities will Isaiah's ideal leader possess?

4. (5 minutes) A volunteer reads **Isaiah 30:15** (page 118) aloud. Students answer the compass question by writing a journal entry.

5. (5 minutes) A volunteer reads **Isaiah 32:16–18** (page 118). Read the compass note. Students compare the words of the rabbis to the words of Isaiah. Students write their own ending to the saying of the rabbis, "The world stands on …"

Experiential Learning: (10 minutes)

Read aloud **Making a Difference** (page 120). Put up a poster board that has columns for the days of the week students are in class. Hand out slips of paper to students and ask them to write down an extra mitzvah they can do each day in class on each slip. Students stick their suggestions on the poster board. Discuss how all the extra mitzvot would improve the class.

Wrapping It Up: (5 minutes)

Discuss how Isaiah's teachings are relevant today.

15 – Jeremiah, the Chosen Prophet, Lesson 1
Essential Question: How do young people guarantee the future of the Jewish nation?

Learning Objectives: Students will be able to:
- Describe the significance of Tisha B'Av.
- Reflect on actions they can take to ensure the future of the Jewish people.
- Explain the messages that Jeremiah relayed to the Jewish people.

Getting Started: (5 minutes) Ask: Why does a traffic light flash before it turns red? List examples of other warnings. Why do we need warnings? Who gives you warnings? In this chapter, students will learn about the prophet Jeremiah who relayed God's warnings to the Jewish people.

Exploring the Text:
1. (5 minutes) Call on a student to read aloud **Jeremiah 1:4 – 8** (page 123). Review what students learned about what it means to be holy (*set apart*). Ask: How does this explain why God tells Jeremiah that he is holy?

2. (20 minutes) Divide students into groups. Groups should assign one member to record their answers and another to create a timeline of events for the sections they will read in the chapter. Students read **Jeremiah 26:1–6** (page 123). Ask: Why is God angry with the priests and the prophets? What does God mean by "my Torah"? Read **By My Torah** on page 124 and discuss the explanation and how it adds to understanding God's words to Jeremiah.

   Groups read **Jeremiah 26:11–16** (page 124). Ask: Why did the priests and prophets object to Jeremiah's words while the people supported him? Why is it difficult to be the one telling people in authority that they are doing wrong?

   Groups read **Jeremiah 32:26–35** (page 124) and **Jeremiah 32:36–40** (page 125). Read the first compass note on page 125 aloud. Ask: Which part of God's message is *din* and which part is *raḥamim*?

   Groups read **Jeremiah 36:1–10** (page 125) and **Jeremiah 36:11–32** (page 125). Ask: Why does Jeremiah send Baruch to the Temple? Compare the people's response with the king's response.

Experiential Learning: (15 minutes)
Read **Jeremiah 38:17–39:8** and **Jeremiah 42:1–12** (page 126) aloud. Inform students that the destruction of Jerusalem in 586 BCE and the forced exile of Jews to Babylonia were major catastrophes for the Jewish people. Students should complete their timelines. Explain that each year, on Tisha B'Av, the anniversary of the destruction of the Temple, Jews remember the tragedy by fasting and reading the Book of Lamentations (traditionally understood to be written by Jeremiah). Seat students in a circle on the floor and give each one a copy of Lamentations. Students take turns reading excerpts (pre-chosen or of their own choosing) aloud. Discuss students' responses to the experience.

Exploring the Text: (5 minutes)
Read **Kid Power** (page 128) aloud. Ask: Why are young people the best guarantors for the Torah? Discuss how by performing mitzvot, students contribute to the future of the Jewish community.

> **Wrapping It Up:** (5 minutes)
> Point out that this lesson concludes the class's study of the Book of Prophets. Based on the stories they read about the prophets, students create a class definition of a Jewish prophet.

16 – **Queen Esther Saves the Jews**, Lesson 1
Essential Question: How are all Jews responsible for one another?

Learning Objectives: Students will be able to:

- Identify the biblical sources for the holiday of Purim.

- Describe what life is like for Jews in other countries.

- Explain how we are all responsible for our fellow Jews.

Getting Started: (5 minutes)

In 1949, as life became increasingly difficult for Jews in Yemen, 49,000 Yemenite Jews were airlifted to Israel in Operation Magic Carpet. Ask: Why would Israel, then a small, new country, take responsibility for all of these people? Emphasize the solidarity of the Jewish people and our shared responsibility to one another. Explain that in this chapter, we will see how Esther acts on behalf of the Jewish community.

Exploring the Text:

1. (20 minutes) Students look at the *Megillah* (Scroll of Esther) on page 134 and read the caption. Review the three parts of Tanach and explain that Esther is found in the Writings section of Tanach. Divide students into groups and assign each group a section of Esther from the textbook. Groups prepare and perform their scenes. Provide students with costumes and props for dressing up in character.

2. (5 minutes) Students make three columns on a piece of paper and add headings for King Ahasuerus, Mordecai, and Queen Esther. In partners, students skim the chapter, listing motivations for each character at different points in the story. Partners analyze their list of motivations and make generalizations (*King Ahaseurus is motivated by the will of others; Mordecai is motivated by Jewish law and the good of the Jewish people*). Students share their generalizations with the class.

3. (5 minutes) Read **All For One** (page 138) aloud. Discuss how this connects to Operation Magic Carpet.

4. (5 Minutes) Students read **Caring Connections** (page 139) independently and write answers to the questions in their journal.

The Tech Connection: (10 minutes)

Partners research different Jewish communities around the world. JewishVirtualLibrary.com is a good source of information. Enter the library's Web site and conduct a search for "Jewish Communities."

Experiential Learning: (10 minutes)

Partners create a poster about their Jewish community and share their findings with the class.

> **Wrapping It Up:** (5 minutes)
> Students write individual responses to the prompt: Queen Esther is a role model for all people because…

17 – Daniel's Risk, Lesson 1
Essential Question: How can we affirm our commitment to our faith?

Learning Objectives: Students will be able to:

- Recount the story of the three men walking out of the fire unhurt.
- Identify Jewish heroes that refused to give up their faith.
- Explain how we can affirm our commitment to our faith.

Getting Started: (5 Minutes)

Students brainstorm a list of people from the Bible or Jewish history who have put their lives in danger in order to keep their commitment to Judaism (*Mordecai, Judah Maccabee*). Discuss contemporary challenges to our faith.

Exploring the Text:

1. (15 minutes) Review the exile of the Jewish people to Babylonia as described at the end of the chapter about Jeremiah. Inform them that Nebuchadnezzar took some Jews to Babylonia before the final exile. Read **Daniel 1:1–2:48** and **Daniel 3:1–20** (page 141) aloud. Ask: What do you think life was like for Jews in Babylonia at this time.

   Students predict what will happen to the three men. Read **Daniel 3:21–33** (page 142) aloud. Students compare **Nebuchadnezzar's** response with that of the king of Nineveh in the story of Jonah. Students discuss what might have happened to the men inside the fire.

   Read **Daniel 5:1–11** (page 143) aloud. Ask: What has Belshazzar done wrong? Who do you think will be called to read the writing on the wall? Read **Daniel 5:13–29** (page 144) aloud. Ask: To whom do you think Belshazzar's kingdom will be given (*Persians*)? Inform students that the clue is in the chapter about Esther.

Experiential Learning: (10 minutes)

Divide students into small groups. Give students the following scenario:

> Students on your soccer team say a distinctly Christian prayer which is led by the coach before each game. The coach and other kids know that you and one other person on the team are Jewish, but they insist that everyone must say the prayer.

Students dramatize the scenario in their group and act out responses.

After each group has done the activity, discuss how students felt during the role-play, whether they felt the scenario was realistic or not, and what conflicting loyalties come into play when dealing with this type of situation.

The Tech Connection: (15 minutes)

Read the caption for the photo on page 142. Inform students that Nebuchadnezzar was a great builder. Partners search the Web for the Pergamon Museum in Berlin to learn about what Nebuchadnezzar built. Students view the images and write a description of what it might have felt like to visit Babylonia in the time of Nebuchadnezzar.

Wrapping It Up: (5 minutes)

Ask: How did different characters in this chapter display their commitment to their faith? How can you learn from their example?

17 – Daniel's Risk, Lesson 2

Essential Question: What is the best way to speak up when others are not acting correctly?

Learning Objectives: Students will be able to:

- Recount events that prompted the foreign kings to praise the God of Israel.

- Identify the languages in which the Book of Daniel is written.

- Explain how we should speak up when others do not act appropriately.

Getting Started: (5 minutes)

Give students the following scenario: In the hallway at school, two students steal an iPod from a third student. A fourth student witnesses this. Ask: What should the eyewitness do? Discuss their answers. In this chapter, students will read about Daniel who was willing to speak up and tell a king that he was acting wrongly.

Exploring the Text:

1. (20 minutes) Divide students into five groups. Each group is assigned one of the paragraphs on pages 144 and 145.

    Groups read and discuss the assigned paragraph together. Groups identify the most important sentence in the paragraph.

    Divide students into a second set of groups, making sure that a representative from each of the original groups is in each new group. Representatives summarize their paragraphs for the rest of the group and direct group attention to the key sentence in the text.

2. (5 minutes) Students read **A New Language** (page 144) independently. Inform them that the language of the prayer Kaddish is Aramaic. Students find the Kaddish in the prayer book and identify the letter that is the most common ending for a word (*aleph*). Explain that *aleph* at the end of an Aramaic word means "the."

Experiential Learning: (15 minutes)

In groups of two or three, students read **Duke of Rebuke** (page 146) and **A Little Sensitivity, Please** (page 147). Give groups slips of paper. Students develop scenarios in which someone is not behaving correctly and write them down on the slips of paper. Put the slips in a paper bag. Groups take one slip and act out the scenario, adding their own ending. Discuss the best ways to rebuke someone.

> **Wrapping It Up:** (5 minutes)
> The title of this chapter is *Daniel's Risk*. Students evaluate whether this is a good title and suggest their own alternate titles for the chapter.

18 – Ezra and Nehemiah Rebuild Jerusalem, Lesson 1

Essential Question: What qualities help us reach our goals?

Learning Objectives: Students will be able to:

- Recount the events surrounding the rebuilding of the Holy Temple.
- Describe the hard work and patience needed to rebuild the Temple.
- Identify different kings who affected the fate of the Jewish people during their exile in Babylonia.

Getting Started: (5 minutes)

Students look at the object and caption on page 150. Ask: What can you infer about the time period of King Cyrus from this cup? Explain that in this chapter, students will learn about a new king, King Cyrus, who would let the Jews return to Jerusalem and rebuild The Temple.

Exploring the Text:

1. (10 minutes) Read **Ezra 1:1–65** (page 149) aloud. Students make four columns on a piece of paper and add headings for King Cyrus, Darius, Nebuchadnezzar, and Belshazzar. Students list differences between the kings. Ask: Which king was best to the Jewish people?

2. (15 minutes) Read the compass note on page 149. Discuss how Persian tolerance of religious diversity may have affected the quality of life for the Jews. Tell students that the Jews had been told by the prophets that the exile would end after seventy years.

   Students imagine that they are living in Persia at this time and are told they may return to Jerusalem and rebuild The Temple. Divide students into two groups — one in favor of returning to Jerusalem and one in favor of staying in Persia. The two groups develop reasons to go or stay and debate the correct course of action. Take a class vote on who would return and who would stay in Persia.

3. (5 minutes) Students read **Ezra 3:10–13** (page 149) independently. Ask: Why did the elders weep? Why were others so happy?

Experiential Learning: (10 minutes)

Students read **Ezra 4:1–6:18** (page 150) independently. Students imagine that they are Jews who have finally finished rebuilding the Temple. One student begins telling the experience of leaving Persia (*I had a good life in Persia. I liked my school…*). Go around the class and have each student add to the story (*…but my Mom said we had to leave and go to Jerusalem…*). Then try another one. Ask: What kind of qualities did it take to leave Persia and go to Jerusalem and rebuild the Temple?

(5 minutes) Students complete **Quality Building Blocks** (page 155) independently. In partners, students compare and contrast their ideas.

Wrapping It Up: (5 minutes)

Students think of a time they reached a goal after a great deal of time and effort. Students share their experiences and feelings about the experiences with the class.

18 – Ezra and Nehemiah Rebuild Jerusalem, Lesson 2

Essential Question: How can we rebuild when something has been lost or destroyed?

Learning Objectives: Students will be able to:
- Recount the events surrounding the rebuilding of the walls of the city of Jerusalem.
- Identify the sources from Ezra and Nehemiah on which the customs for our Torah service are based.
- Explain what it takes to rebuild a place.

Getting Started: (5 minutes)
Students tell what they know of natural disasters that have occurred in the last decade. Discuss the hard work and determination that goes into rebuilding places after these disasters, such as in New Orleans. Explain to students that in this chapter they will learn about Nehemiah and Ezra, who helped rebuild Jerusalem physically and spiritually.

Exploring the Text:
1. (5 minutes) Partners read **Nehemiah 1:1–2:9** (page 151).

Experiential Learning: (10 minutes)
Partners create a poster to inspire more Jews to join Nehemiah's mission. The poster may include text, pictures, and slogans. Put up the posters in the classroom.

Exploring the Text:
2. (10 minutes) Students read **Nehemiah 2:11–18** (page 151), **Nehemiah 3:1–4:7** (page 151), and **Nehemiah 4:8–17** independently. Ask: How do we know that the Jews believed it was up to both them and God to protect Jerusalem?

   Read the compass text on page 151 aloud. Students evaluate whether or not this is a fitting name for Nehemiah. Students suggest other names for Nehemiah.

3. (5 minutes) Read **Nehemiah 8:1–6** (page 152) aloud and locate the origin of the following customs for Torah reading:
   - reciting a blessing before reading from the Torah
   - standing when the Torah is removed from the Ark
   - lifting the Torah scroll for all to see.

4. Read **Nehemiah 8:7–9** (page 152) and answer the compass question.

5. (5 minutes) Students read **Something to Write Home About** (page 153) silently and complete the activity individually.

The Tech Connection: (10 minutes) Read **The Courage to Start Again** (page 154) aloud. Divide students into small groups. Give each group a relief organization to research on the internet such as the International Red Cross, Habitat for Humanity, and Joint Distribution Committee. Groups create Power Point slides explaining the difficult task of emergency relief and how their organization handles it.

Wrapping It Up: (5 minutes)
Students generate a list of biblical characters they learned about that they admire most. Discuss their choices. Students write a journal entry about the one they like best and give reasons for their choice.

ASSESSMENT

Assessing student learning and understanding is an essential part of the teaching process. Assessment is an ongoing process that allows you to gauge the skills and knowledge students gained and identify the lessons that are most effective. It also helps you evaluate whether lessons meet student skill levels and enables you to monitor each student's progress.

Each lesson in this manual includes learning objectives for measurable skills. Checking for these skills is one method of assessment. Other suggestions include:

- Students keep a portfolio of their writing, art, and personal reflections. This methodology of assessment allows you to track individual growth.

- End each class by allowing students to write, draw, create, or tell at least three new facts or concepts they gained from the lesson

- Evaluate the performance-based activities such as oral reports, journal writings, or art activities to assess student knowledge and understanding.

- Ask a variety of questions, such as the ones suggested in the lessons, which call for students to demonstrate their understanding of the texts and their ability to apply the information.

- Include opportunities for student self-assessment in which students answer questions such as: What was the most interesting part of this lesson to you? What was the most challenging part? What questions do you have about the material? Self assessment may be written or oral.

- Students fill out group assessment forms in which they judge how well their group worked together and how much they contributed to the group.

- End each class by having students tell you one new thing they learned in the lesson. The responses will help you assess which aspects of the lesson made the biggest impact on the most students. This also serves as a review of the lesson for the entire class.